JANES IN LOVE

Published by DC Comics,
1700 Broadway, New York, NY 10019.

Printed in Canada.
DC Comics, a Warner Bros.
Entertainment Company.

ISBN: 978-1-4012-1387-9

JANES  in LOVE

by **CECIL CASTELLUCCI**
and **JIM RUGG**

with lettering by **Rob Clark Jr.**
and gray tones by **Jasen Lex**

5

SOMETIMES, I CAN'T BELIEVE HOW NORMAL MY LIFE SEEMS.

BUT ONCE IN A WHILE, IN MY DREAMS, IT'S HAPPENING AGAIN.

8

9

12

14

15

21

24

IN THE METRO CITY HOSPITAL LAST YEAR, AFTER THE ATTACK, IT WAS THE SMELL OF FLOWERS THAT HELPED GET RID OF THE SMELL OF SMOKE.

SMELL IS SO POWERFUL.

DO YOU NEED ANOTHER PILLOW?

I CAN RING THE NURSE IF YOU WANT.

OH, JANE. *PLEASE* TALK TO ME.

MY MOM HAS A BOOK CALLED "THE SECRET MEANING OF FLOWERS."

IT SAYS MUMS MEAN HOPE.

MOM USED TO BRING ME MUMS ALL THE TIME.

27

28

THERE'S NOTHING LIKE GETTING A PACKAGE IN THE MAIL.

YOU WAIT AND WAIT AND WAIT FOR IT AND WHEN IT COMES, YOU REALIZE THAT THERE COULD BE ANYTHING IN THERE.

YOUR EXPECTATIONS MIGHT BE TOO HIGH.

SO, YOU ARE HOPEFUL, BUT CAUTIOUS.

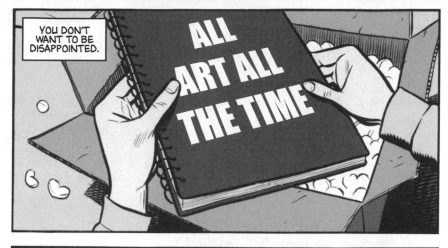

31

DeAr JANE

Hello. How wonderful to be able to say these words to you.
Hello, dear Jane. Light of my life.

Slow is the world
I have to take things
At a slower pace
Thoughts like molasses
Careful steps
Cautious
When I speak I slur
And the soup my mother feeds me
Dribbles out the left corner of my mouth.
I am safe now
Back again in the world of light

They tell me that you took your coat off

And held my bleeding leg with all your might

Did not let go

But kept the pressure on

Until help arrived.

They say you would not leave me

Until you were told

The bleeding was under control

I remember nothing

But a beautiful blue day

And a cappuccino

That came with foam pressed in the pattern of a leaf

I hadn't but taken two sips

When the world slowed down

I remember singing
Row, row, row your boat
With a sweet voice
I learned it in English class
And knew the words
As things went black
And I went gently down the stream

Thank you ♥

NAME: _Doe J_
SEX: M
BED: 1174B
DATE: 8/6/07

34

35

36

37

40

41

42

43

44

ONE JANE DOWN, MEANS IT'S EASY TO GET SLOPPY.

I WAS THINKING ABOUT OTHER THINGS. SO, I DIDN'T SEE IT COMING.

51

52

53

54

56

59

61

I AM GLAD YOU GOT COMMUNITY SERVICE, FOR P.L.A.I.N.

MAYBE IT WILL MAKE YOU THINK *TWICE* ABOUT THE HARM AND WORRY YOU'RE CAUSING, JANE.

I WILL. I PROMISE.

ONE OF THE REASONS I WANT TO MAKE THE WORLD BEAUTIFUL IS SO THAT MY MOM CAN REMEMBER IT IS.

BUT MAYBE YOU CAN'T MAKE THE WORLD BEAUTIFUL FOR ANYONE.

MAYBE IT'S BEST IF I CONCENTRATE ON BEING A NORMAL GIRL.

MAYBE THEN NO ONE WOULD GET INTO TROUBLE.

I COULD HAVE A CRUSH ON A MOVIE STAR.

SHOP FOR TRENDY CLOTHES.

LET MY HAIR GO BLONDE AGAIN.

MAYBE THE OLD ME IS THE SAFER GIRL TO BE.

JANE BECKLES
90 ASHWOOD ROAD
KENT WATERS, NY 14054

68

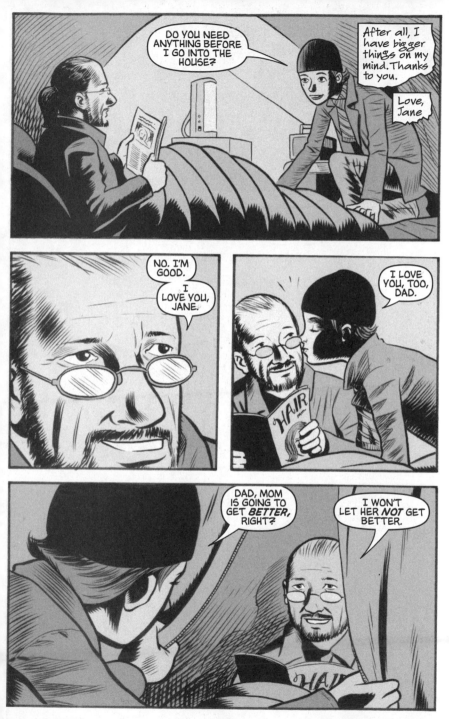

70

COMING SOON
WATER PARK ESTATES

FINAL FARMER MARKET TODAY 3 PM

COMING SOON AT THIS SITE WATER PARK ESTATES CONDOS

WHY DO PEOPLE WANT TO GET RID OF THE THINGS THAT ARE GOOD IN THE WORLD? THE THINGS THAT BRING PEOPLE TOGETHER?

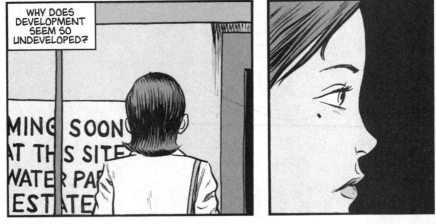

WHY DOES DEVELOPMENT SEEM SO UNDEVELOPED?

MING SOON AT THS SITE WATER PA ESTATE

AUDREY, WHAT WILL YOU DO NOW THAT THEY'RE CLOSING THE MARKET?

IT'S HARD TO START OVER AT *MY* AGE.

OH, THERE YOU ARE, DAMON.

DO YOU KNOW JANE?

HI, DAMON.

HI, JANE.

I'VE SEEN DAMON A MILLION TIMES...

BUT WHEN HE SNEAKS UP ON ME, EVEN IF IT'S COLD OUTSIDE...

I MELT.

JANE CAN HELP YOU CARRY THE ORDER TO THE CAR, DAMON. THE SUNSET HALL BOUGHT THE REST OF MY STOCK.

WELL, IT WAS MR. YAMAMOTO'S IDEA. HE'S GOING TO MISS GETTING A FLOWER FOR HIS LAPEL.

MR. YAMAMOTO. SUCH A GENTLEMAN. KNOWS HIS FLOWERS. IMPECCABLE TASTE. KIND HEART. GOOD SOUL.

HERE COMES TROUBLE.

YOU TWO ARE SOME KIND OF SNEAKY *PUNKS,* AREN'T YOU? I SAID NO PUBLIC ART. AND I MEANT IT. I'LL *UP* YOUR PUNISHMENTS IF YOU KEEP AT IT.

WHAT IS HE TALKING ABOUT?

BEATS ME. HE PROBABLY SAW A PILE OF TIRES AND THOUGHT IT WAS ART.

LIKE MARCEL DUCHAMP. I *LOVE* DADA!

I KNOW WHAT HE'S REFERRING TO...

83

85

MY FAVE METRO CITY ARTIST, DINO SALAR, SAYS THAT YOUR ANGST IS YOUR CANVAS. PAINT WIDE..

THAT'S THE KINDA THING THAT CAN GET YOU AN ARTS GRANT.

I COULD DO THIS. MAYBE.

HEY, JANE, WHAT'S THAT?

HEY. PRIVATE!

KASUMI WORKS AT THE SUNSET HOUSE.

SHE'S OLD. LIKE 25.

WE'RE TRYING TO FIGURE OUT HOW TO HOOK UP MR. YAMAMOTO AND AUDREY.

SOMETIMES I THINK WE'RE JUST FRIENDS.

GOOD PROJECT.

94

Congratulations, Jane Beckles. Your group P.L.A.I.N. People Loving Art In Neighborhoods: The Universe is a Garden project has been selected for round two of the grant application process. Please present yourself and your group's portfolio on Saturday, February 20th at the offices of the National Foundation for the American Arts at 2:30 PM for an interview regarding your project.

I DID IT!

MAKING THE INTERVIEW MEANS CUTTING SCHOOL ON FRIDAY.

BUT FATE SOMETIMES HAS A WAY OF MAKING SURE THAT YOU HAVE A FRIEND ALONG WITH YOU--

JANE!

--WHEN YOU'RE GOING TO DO SOMETHING SCARY.

HAVE YOU COME HERE TO MOCK ME?

TO TELL ME THAT RHYS IS JUST A *FIGMENT* OF MY IMAGINATION?

METRO CITY IS BIG. YOU MIGHT NEED A FRIEND. AND I HAVE AN ERRAND TO RUN...

THE LAND OUTSIDE THE WINDOW CHANGES DRAMATICALLY.

ROUGH.

WILD.

CULTIVATED.

DESOLATE.

I DON'T DOUBT THAT IT'S LIKE OUR CHANGING NATURE.

THE WHEELS ARE STEADY, LIKE THE RHYTHM OF OUR HEARTS.

NATIONAL FOUNDATION FOR THE AMERICAN ARTS

DO YOU WANT TO TALK ABOUT WHAT HAPPENED WITH RHYS?

NO. LET'S JUST GET THROUGH YOUR INTERVIEW AND THEN GO HOME.

I'LL WAIT OUTSIDE.

...SO, AS YOU CAN SEE, THIS EMPTY LOT WOULD SERVE OUR ART COLLECTIVE'S PURPOSES WELL...

My BODY IS BEAUTIFUL!

Group Strikes Again

WHO WOULD YOU COMPARE YOUR WORK TO?

I WOULD COMPARE OUR WORK TO DINO SALAR, BUT I THINK HE'S KIND OF LOST HIS *EDGE* LATELY.

I AM DINO SALAR. I DON'T THINK I'VE LOST MY EDGE.

OH, GOD. I'VE ALREADY BLOWN IT.

NOXIOUS ODOR...

ATTACK...

TERRORISTS...

IT'S NOT DANGEROUS. IT'S JUST A PHEROMONE.

SO, JAYNE, WHO ARE YOUR "FRIENDS"?

KENT WATERS WAS SO ON EDGE THAT EVERY LITTLE THING SET THEM OFF.

OK, BOYS, MOVE ALONG.

THEY FOLLOWED ME OUT HERE.

117

125

It's amazing how your parents can totally come through for you when they can see how hard you're working for something.

No parent wants to see their kid lose the good fight.

I FOUND US ALL TRENCH COATS. THE SIZES MIGHT BE A LITTLE WONKY BUT THEY'LL DO.

I'll tell you how it goes. Love, Jane.

DO I *REALLY* HAVE TO WEAR THIS?

IF YOU STILL WANT TO DATE ME YOU DO.

ALL RIGHT THEN.

I'LL TAKE CARE OF THE DJ. HE'S ON STAGE CREW WITH ME.

SO COATS ON UNTIL THE SONG COMES ON. THEN WE DO IT.

THIS IS GOING TO BE THE BEST *DANCE* EVER.

128

129

132

133

134

138

139

140

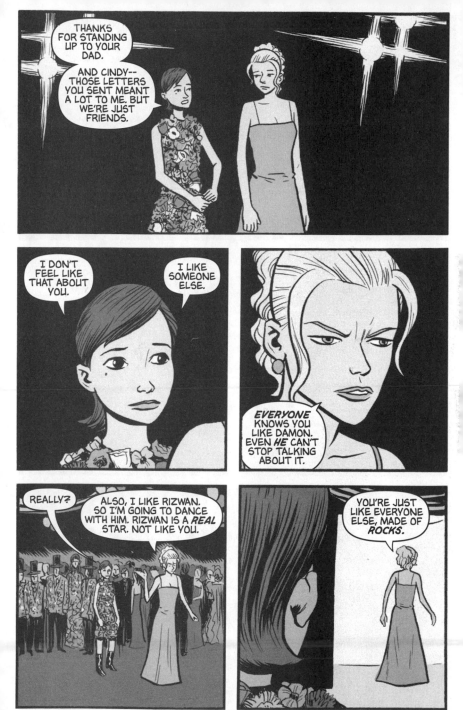

142

145

You are cordially invited to the Universe is a Garden Project Opening to take place on the summer solstice Saturday, June 21 please arrive when the sun sets and the stars rise
The Kent
enage Artis
eckles, once an artistic outlaw, is now a source of pride for the town of Kent Waters. The group she founded, along with other Buzz Aldrin High School students, has put the town on the radar of the National Arts Council with a grant to fund the project The Universe is A Garden. "I was inspired by the empty lot and the old farmers market," Miss Beckles said. "It seemed like we needed a beautiful space in that lot. I like to make things beautiful." Townsfolk will surely remember some of P.L.A.I.N.'s more notable projects, the marionettes, the chalk

150

Photo by Andrew Takeuchi

CECIL CASTELLUCCI

Cecil grew up in New York City. She's the author of three young adult novels, *Boy Proof*, *The Queen of Cool* and *Beige*. Her books have received starred reviews and been on the American Library Association's Best Books for Young Adults (BBYA), Quick Pick for Reluctant Readers, Great Graphic Novels for Teens and the Amelia Bloomer lists. In 2008, she won the Joe Shuster Award for Outstanding Canadian Comic Book Writer. Cecil is also a playwright, a filmmaker and an erstwhile indie rock musician. She looks for street art whenever she's on a walk. Currently her favorite street artist is Banksy. She splits her time between Los Angeles and the East Coast.

JIM RUGG

Jim grew up and continues t
reside near Pittsburgh with
his wife and three cats.
He's the co-creator of
Street Angel and *Afrodisiac*
His work has appeared in
Project: Superior, *Project:*
Romantic, *SPX2005*, *Orchid*,
Meathaus, *VH1*, and the
Society of Illustrators
Annual.

ECIAL PREVIEW OF THE GRAPHIC NOVELS THAT WILL DEFINE 2008

minx

ur life. Your books.
How novel.

token

by alisa kwitney and joëlle jones

Written by noted comics writer and noveli[st]
ALISA KWITNEY

Can a Jewish "girl out of time" and a Spanish old soul survive culture clashes and

criminal records to find true love in the sun-drenched, sequined miasma that was

South Beach in the Big '80s?

By ALISA KWITNEY & JOËLLE JONES
AVAILABLE IN OCTOBER ■ Read on.

But I CAN imagine Ocean Drive the way it once was, back in the thirties and forties.

Women in silk gowns, walking barefoot on the sand. Men in tuxedos, asking if you want some ice with your champagne.

Say "yes" and they throw a DIAMOND in your drink.

SHIRAAAAA!!!

But this is 1987, and South Beach and most of its inhabitants are WAY past their prime.

The New York Four
Brian Wood + Ryan Kelly

Written by multiple Eisner Award
nominee/indie icon BRIAN WOOD

Experience New York City through the eyes of Riley, a shy, almost reclusive straight-A

student who convinces three other NYU freshmen to join a research group to earn

extra money.

As the girls become fast friends, two things complicate what should be the greatest

time of Riley's life: connecting with her arty, estranged older sister and having a

mysterious online crush on a guy known only as "sneakerfreak."

By BRIAN WOOD & RYAN KELLY

Broadway & Houston Streets.
(NY 101: If you pronounced it like Houston, Texas, you are most likely a tourist. Say "house-tin" instead.)

(This is drop-dead downtown New York City. Walk east to the Lower East Side, west for the Village, south for Soho, or north towards the NYU campus, which is where Riley's headed.)

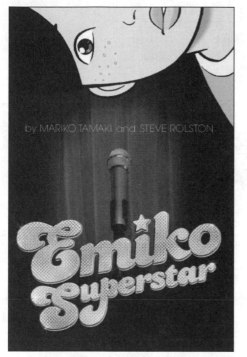

Written by novelist/performance artist
MARIKO TAMAKI

A "borrowed" diary, a double life and identity issues fuel a teenager's quest to find

herself before she cracks and commits social suicide. Watch Emi go from dull

suburban babysitter to eclectic urban performance artist — compliments of one

crazy summer.

By MARIKO TAMAKI & STEVE ROLSTON
AVAILABLE IN SEPTEMBER ■ Read on.

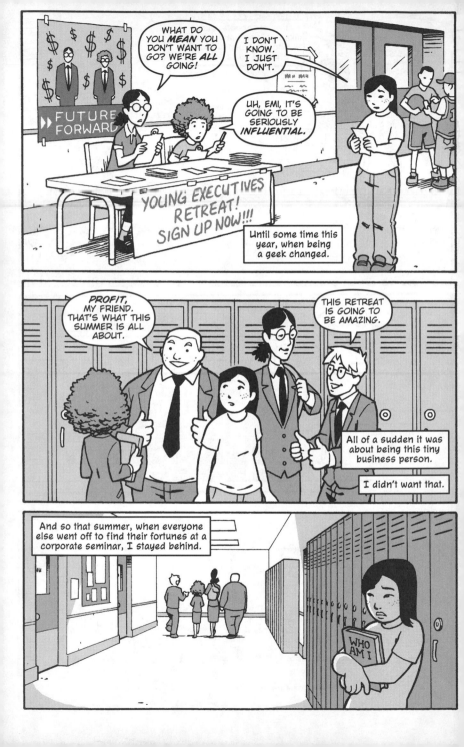

Your life in pictures starts here!

~A DO-IT YOURSELF MINI COMIC~

Write your story ideas here:

Draw your main character sketches here:

Use the following 3 pages to bring it all together.

TITLE: BY:

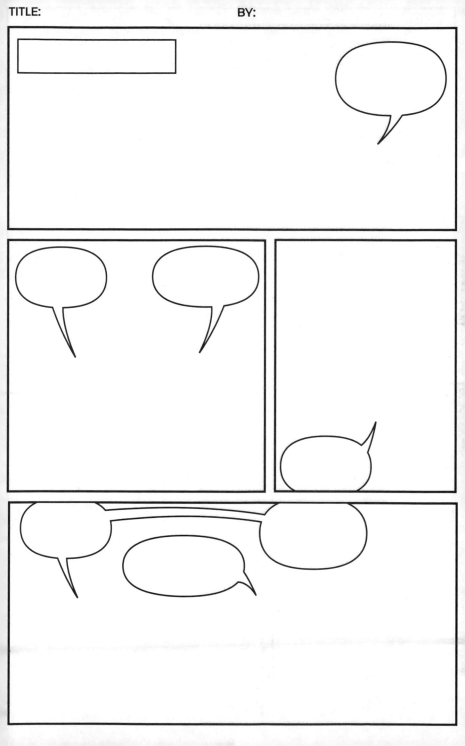